Cambridge English

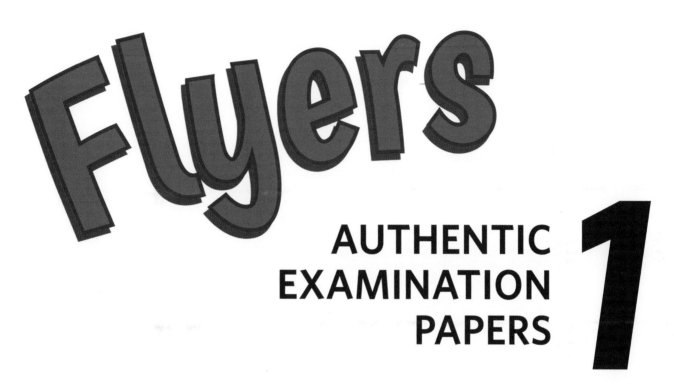

Flyers

AUTHENTIC EXAMINATION PAPERS

1

STUDENT'S BOOK

Cambridge University Press
www.cambridge.org/elt

Cambridge Assessment English
www.cambridgeenglish.org

Information on this title: www.cambridge.org/9781316635919

© Cambridge University Press and UCLES 2017

First published 2017

22 21 20

Printed in Malaysia by Vivar Printing

A catalogue record for this publication is available from the British Library

ISBN 978-1-316-63591-9 Student's Book
ISBN 978-1-316-63595-7 Answer Booklet
ISBN 978-1-316-63599-5 Audio CD

Cover illustration: (T) IvanNikulin/iStock/Getty Images Plus; (B) adekvat/iStock/Getty Images Plus

<u>Contents</u>

Part 1
– 5 questions –

Listen and draw lines. There is one example.

Vicky   Tom   Richard   Katy

Clare   Paul   David

Part 2
– 5 questions –

Listen and write. There is one example.

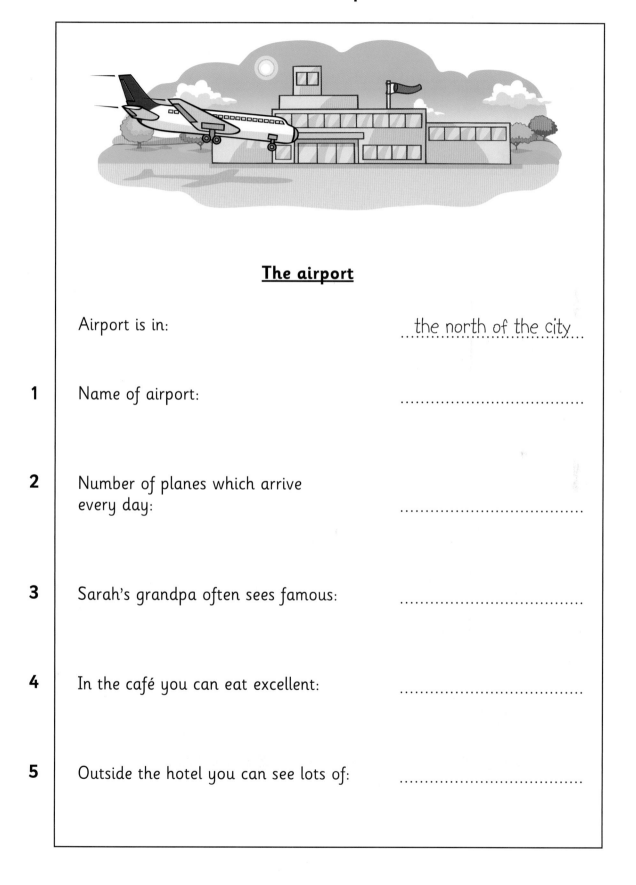

The airport

Airport is in: ....the north of the city..........

1 Name of airport: ....

2 Number of planes which arrive
every day: ....

3 Sarah's grandpa often sees famous: ....

4 In the café you can eat excellent: ....

5 Outside the hotel you can see lots of: ....

Part 3

– 5 questions –

Where did Harry's grandma take pictures of these people?

Listen and write a letter in each box. There is one example.

Grandpa — A

Lucy — ☐

Jane — ☐

William — ☐

Oliver — ☐

Sophia — ☐

A

B

C

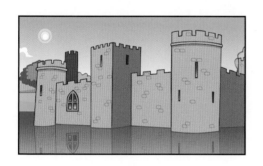

D

E

F

G

H

Part 4

– 5 questions –

Listen and tick (✔) the box. There is one example.

Where will Helen's club meet on Saturday?

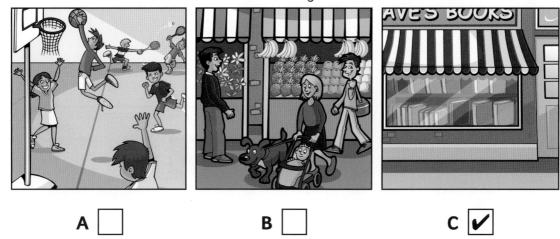

A ☐   B ☐   C ✔

1   What does Helen play at the club?

A ☐   B ☐   C ☐

2   What must Helen take to the club this week?

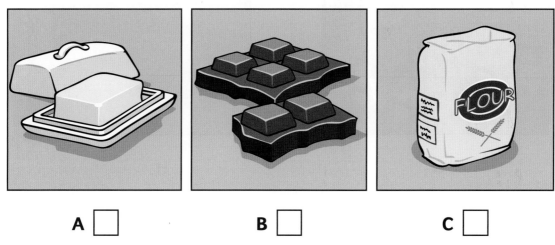

A ☐   B ☐   C ☐

3   Who's going to visit the club next month?

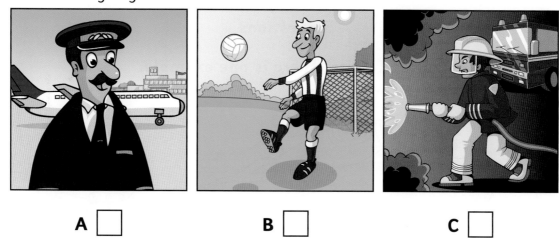

A ☐   B ☐   C ☐

4   Which film was the most interesting?

A ☐   B ☐   C ☐

5   What is the club going to do on holiday next year?

A ☐   B ☐   C ☐

Part 5
– 5 questions –

Listen and colour and write. There is one example.

To the
_____

Reading and Writing

Part 1

– 10 questions –

Look and read. Choose the correct words and write them on the lines. There is one example.

flour   police stations   honey   singers

These people wear special clothes and travel in rockets to go into space.   astronauts

cereal   **1**   The people who work in these make things like toys or televisions. ....   a bank

2   The people who work here wear uniforms and sometimes help with traffic problems. ....

3   This is usually made of tomatoes, cheese and other things on top of a kind of bread. ....

sugar   **4**   If you want to work here you must be very good at counting money. ....   artists

5   A person with this job brings food and drink to your table when you go out for a meal. ....

factories   **6**   These places often have thousands of seats. They are usually full when there is an important football match. ....   salt

7   This is a popular food at breakfast and people usually put milk on it. ....

8   We get this white food from the sea and people put it on their food with pepper. ....

a waiter   **9**   You can go to see famous paintings by these people in museums. ....   astronauts

10 Some people put this in yoghurt, bees make it and it's sweet. ....

a pizza   theatres   stadiums

Part 2

– 5 questions –

Helen is talking to a man about his castle. What does the man say?

Read the conversation and choose the best answer.
Write a letter (A–H) for each answer.

You do not need to use all the letters. There is one example.

Example

Helen: Please can I ask you some questions about your castle? It's for my homework.

Man: ....C..................

Questions

1 **Helen:** Your castle is lovely! Have you lived here for a long time?

   Man: ....

2 **Helen:** Does the castle have an interesting history?

   Man: ....

3 **Helen:** Have you ever felt afraid in the castle?

   Man: ....

4 **Helen:** Lots of people visit your home, don't they?

   Man: ....

5 **Helen:** Who cleans the castle?

   Man: ....

A	My wife and I do that for three hours a day. It's a big job.
B	I came here when I was four or five years old.
C	Of course you can. I'm happy to help. **(Example)**
D	Only twice, when I heard strange sounds which I don't like.
E	Me too. It's very quiet here because we live in the countryside.
F	Oh yes! A famous queen lived here in the sixteenth century.
G	I can't remember but it's very old.
H	We enjoy having them here and learning about this important place.

Part 3
– 6 questions –

Read the story. Choose a word from the box. Write the correct word next to numbers 1–5. There is one example.

Example				
island	slowly	foggy	minutes	broken
else	once	spring	tried	believe

Katy and Fred went to stay with their cousin, David, who lives on an

.............island............. . They wanted to see the whales which visited

there just **(1)** .... a year. On the second day, David's

dad took the children down to the beach to look for whales. The children

were very excited. They waited for a long time, but no whales came.

Then the weather got **(2)** .... so they went home.

They did this for three days but they didn't see any whales.

On the fifth day, they **(3)** .... again. They sat on

some rocks in the sun. Katy said, 'It doesn't matter if we don't see any

whales because I'm so happy!' Then Katy started singing. After a few

(4) ...., several whales appeared. David's dad

shouted, 'Look! They heard you sing and they are coming to listen! I don't

(5) .... it.' The animals came very near to them.

But when Katy stopped singing they swam away again while the children

waved goodbye.

(6)   Now choose the best name for the story.

Tick one box.

The ship and the whales   ☐

The day the whales arrived   ☐

Some whales sing a song   ☐

Part 4
– 10 questions –

Read the text. Choose the right words and write them on the lines.

Farms

Example There are farms ....in...................... all parts of the world.

There are small ones and big ones. Farms are very important

1 .... we get a lot of our food from them.

2 .... farmers grow fruit and vegetables only. In

3 hot countries, these farmers grow things .... rice,

mangoes and bananas, which need a lot of sun. In colder countries,

4 farmers grow carrots, onions and apples. ....

5 farmers have animals. Farmers keep .... to sell

their meat, wool and milk.

6 Farmers have to work very hard .... day of the

7 year. They must .... their animals and water the

things they are growing.

Farmers need to know about the weather every day. If

8 .... is too much sun, the ground gets very dry

9 and things .... grow. Too much rain is also bad

for the fields.

10 .... farmers don't only look after animals, but

they fix their farm machines and tractor engines as well.

Example	on	in	at
1	after	because	so
2	Some	Any	Both
3	through	like	than
4	Other	Another	Each
5	they	their	them
6	every	all	many
7	feed	fed	feeding
8	he	it	there
9	can't	shouldn't	mustn't
10	Most	Few	Any

Part 5

– 7 questions –

Look at the picture and read the story. Write some words to complete the sentences about the story. You can use 1, 2, 3 or 4 words.

The great day

Last Wednesday morning, Daisy got out of bed and looked out of her bedroom window. There was snow everywhere. It looked amazing. Daisy ran quickly to tell her brother, Jim.

Downstairs in the kitchen Mum said, 'I've phoned the school. It's closed today!' The children were very happy. They texted their friends and they all agreed to meet at 10 o'clock in the park.

After breakfast, Jim and Daisy's mum gave them some biscuits to take with them. They said goodbye, and then they ran to the park. In the park, they looked for their friends. Something hit Jim on his shoulder. They turned round and saw their five friends with snowballs in their hands. Jim and Daisy picked up some snow, and threw snowballs back. They spent three hours playing like this. Then they stopped and ate Mum's biscuits.

Next the children got lots of snow and with this they made a big snowman. They put a hat and scarf on it and used small pieces of wood for its face. Then Jim took a photo of his friends next to the snowman.

Next morning when the children looked, there was no snow near their house. There was only a little at the top of the hills just outside their town. So they got ready, cycled to school and chatted about their great day in the snow.

Examples

It was ....*last Wednesday*.......... when Daisy saw snow out of her window.

The snow made everywhere look ....*amazing*.................. .

Questions

1   Mum .... and found out it was closed.

2   Jim, Daisy and their friends decided to go to the park
    at ....

3   A snowball hit Jim's .... when he and Daisy
    arrived at the park.

4   The children played with snowballs for ....

5   After eating the .... , the children made a
    snowman.

6   They gave the snowman a face which was made
    of ....

7   Next morning, the children could only see snow on the
    .... near their town.

Part 6

– 5 questions –

Read the letter and write the missing words. Write one word on each line.

	Dear Mr White
Example	Last Sunday I ....was............. walking in the forest
	with my dog when she found a box in the ground.
	It was difficult but I opened the box. I saw a letter inside, so I
1	got the letter out and .... it carefully.
2	When I looked .... the address and
	date, I couldn't believe your home is so far away! And you
3	hid the box in the forest 30 years ....
	I am very happy that I have found a new friend
4	.... lives in another city.
5	Please write and .... me about your
	family and your country.
	Ben Hill

Part 7

Look at the three pictures. Write about this story. Write **20 or** more words.

....

....

....

....

....

....

Listening

Part 1
– 5 questions –

Listen and draw lines. There is one example.

Daisy   Robert   Paul   Betty

Charlie   Katy   Sally

Part 2

– 5 questions –

Listen and write. There is one example.

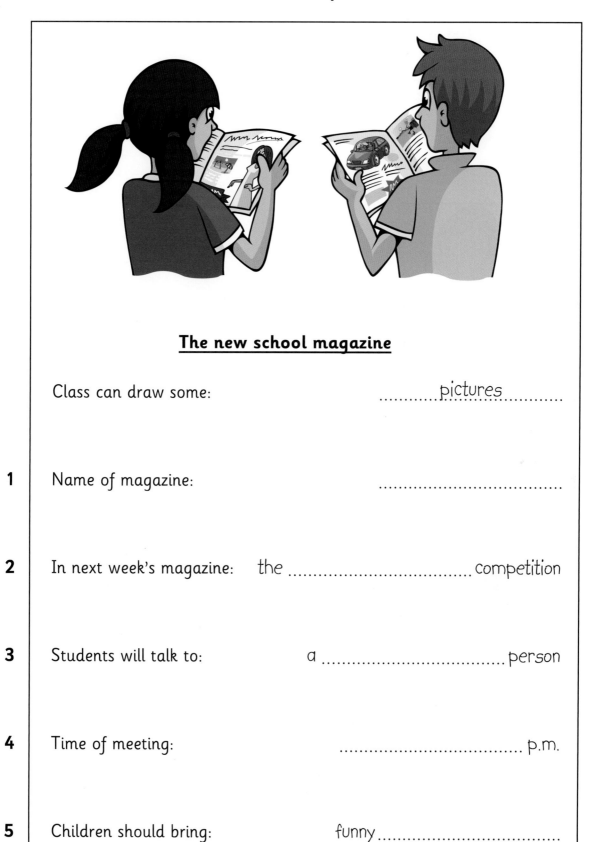

The new school magazine

	Class can draw some:	...........pictures...........
1	Name of magazine:	....
2	In next week's magazine:	the .... competition
3	Students will talk to:	a .... person
4	Time of meeting:	.... p.m.
5	Children should bring:	funny ....

Part 3
– 5 questions –

Where did each person go?

Listen and write a letter in each box. There is one example.

Richard   [E]

Helen   [ ]

Jim   [ ]

Lucy   [ ]

Oliver   [ ]

Jane   [ ]

A

B

C

D

E

F

G

H

Part 4
– 5 questions –

Listen and tick (✔) the box. There is one example.

What time does Harry's family have to leave the house?

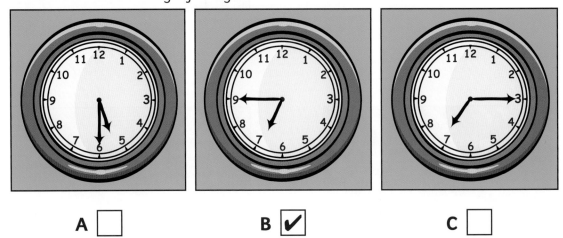

A ☐   B ✔   C ☐

1 What must Harry take on holiday?

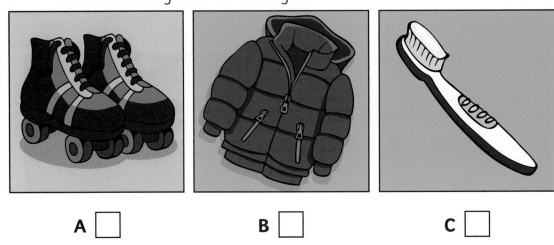

A ☐   B ☐   C ☐

2 Where is Harry's diary?

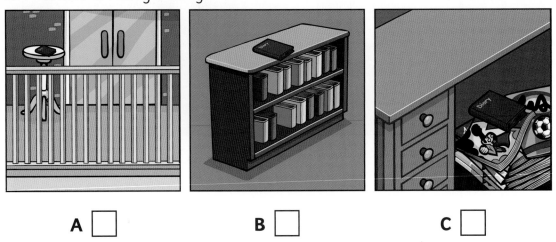

A ☐   B ☐   C ☐

3   Where would Harry most like to go?

A ☐   B ☐   C ☐

4   What animal did Harry's family film last year?

A ☐   B ☐   C ☐

5   What is Harry's mum going to buy?

A ☐   B ☐   C ☐

Part 5

– 5 questions –

Listen and colour and write. There is one example

Reading and Writing

Part 1

– 10 questions –

Look and read. Choose the correct words and write them on the lines. There is one example.

jam   actors   a firefighter   a flashlight

an astronaut

cheese

a cook

a ring

This is usually round and hot with tomatoes on top.	......a pizza......	
1 People need to eat this white food. We get it from the sea and it tastes nice on chips.	....	flour
2 If you have problems with your car, you take it to this person.	....	
3 This is usually made of silver or gold and you can wear it on your finger.	....	
4 It's this person's job to make meals for other people.	....	salt
5 This is often red and is made from fruit and sugar. People put it on bread.	....	
6 You carry this to help you see where you are walking on a dark night.	....	a mechanic
7 You can use this when you want to have tidy hair.	....	
8 This person has learned to fly a rocket into space.	....	
9 These people are good at painting and other people buy their pictures.	....	a pizza
10 This is usually yellow. You might need a knife to cut a piece to put in a sandwich.	....	

a spoon   a comb   artists

Part 2

– 5 questions –

Robert is talking to Helen. What do they say?

Read the conversation and choose the best answer.
Write a letter (A–H) for each answer.

You do not need to use all the letters. There is one example.

Example		
Robert:	Hello Helen. Where are you going?	
Helen:	....................D....................	

Questions

1 **Robert:** Is it your birthday today?

   Helen: ....

2 **Helen:** I'm going to get a new computer game.

   Robert: ....

3 **Helen:** I haven't got many games. Have you?

   Robert: ....

4 **Helen:** Which shop do you think is the best for computer games?

   Robert: ....

5 **Helen:** Would you like to come with us?

   Robert: ....

   Helen: Of course!

A   Yes lots! My favourite one's called 'Music Man'.

B   Me too! Why don't you try them?

C   OK, but I need to phone my parents first.

D   To the shops with my dad. He's going to buy me a birthday present. **(Example)**

E   No, it's next week.

F   You could try the big new one in Swing Road.

G   I love playing those, but it's difficult to stop sometimes.

H   Sorry, I don't. He will be ready in 5 minutes.

Part 3
– 6 questions –

Read the story. Choose a word from the box. Write the correct word next to numbers 1–5. There is one example.

Example				
beach	pushed	ice	temperature	watch
warm	many	took	leave	bored

David's flat is very near the ....beach.......... . He can sit on the

balcony and **(1)** .... all the people who are having

fun in the water. David loves the sea, and often swims in the morning,

before he goes to school. But he usually does that in the summer when the

water's nice and **(2)** ....

But one cold December day in the winter school holidays, David sat

on the sofa and looked at the sea. 'I've nothing to do. I'm so **(3)**

.... ,' he thought. 'I know! The water might be very

cold but I'll go for a swim!'

It only **(4)** .... David two minutes to put on his

swimming shorts, find a large towel and run across the sand to the sea.

He slowly put one foot in the water and quickly pulled it out again!

'David! What are you doing?' his mother called from the flat. 'I want
to go swimming, Mum!' David answered. 'But the sea is colder than

(5) ....! I'll go to the new swimming pool in town
instead! Bye!'

(6)   Now choose the best name for the story.

Tick one box.

David loses his swimming things	☐
David wants a winter swim	☐
Mum goes to the new swimming pool	☐

Part 4

– 10 questions –

Read the text. Choose the right words and write them on the lines.

Lizards

Example | There are about 5000 different kinds ....of............ lizard in
1 | the world. Most lizards are small .... to sit on a
2 | person's hand. .... biggest kind looks more like a
3 | crocodile, and is .... a 'Komodo Dragon'. Lizards
4 | that live in trees or in grass are usually green ....
| lizards that live in deserts are grey or yellow. Most have four legs
5 | and a long tail. Sometimes a lizard loses ....
| tail. But another one will usually grow later. Lizards have very
| short necks, and ears on the outside of their heads. Some people
6 | .... they are ugly! Lizards see different colours
7 | and are very good at .... the quietest sound. They
8 | climb .... trees or over rocks very quickly and
| some can run across water too. Small lizards eat insects. Bigger lizards
9 | catch birds or other small animals to eat. A ....
| lizards only eat plants. Lizards quickly get cold, so most live in hot
10 | countries, ... they can lie in the sun all day.

Example	from	for	of
1	each	enough	else
2	The	A	Every
3	call	calling	called
4	when	after	but
5	our	its	your
6	think	thinks	thinking
7	hearing	hears	hear
8	with	up	until
9	much	both	few
10	why	where	what

Part 5
– 7 questions –

Look at the picture and read the story. Write some words to complete the sentences about the story. You can use 1, 2, 3 or 4 words.

Richard paints his room

Purple was Richard's favourite colour. He had a purple school bag, a purple sweater and his uncle gave him a purple tent for his eleventh birthday!

One day, he said to his mother, 'The walls in my bedroom have been yellow since you painted them when I was five years old, but I'd like to paint them purple now. Can we do that?'

'It's a very dark colour, Richard,' she said. 'If you want a different colour, how about orange? That's nicer, I think!'

'But I love purple, Mum. I'm sure it will look amazing!' Richard answered. 'OK!' his mother said. 'We can fetch some paint from the supermarket. We can buy brushes there too.'

They took the train into the city and got everything that they needed. When they arrived home, they put on some old clothes, carried Richard's bed and cupboards into another room, found some old newspapers and put them on the floor and then started painting. They painted for three hours!

Then they tidied the room, went downstairs and made a hot drink. But Richard was excited and ran upstairs to look at his room again.

'Do you like it?' his mother called from the kitchen.

'It looks great, Mum! I love it!' Richard answered. 'And I'd like to paint my bed and cupboards purple now too, I think!'

Examples

Richard's favourite colour was .... purple ....

On Richard's eleventh birthday, ... his uncle .... gave him a
purple tent.

Questions

1   Richard was .... when his mum painted his
     bedroom yellow.

2   Richard's mother thought .... was a nicer colour
     for his room.

3   They decided to go and get the paint and some new
     .... from the supermarket.

4   They went to the city by .... to do their
     shopping.

5   Richard and his mother put .... on the floor of
     Richard's room before they started painting the walls.

6   They spent .... painting the room.

7   Richard wanted his .... to be purple next!

Part 6
– 5 questions –

Read the diary and write the missing words. Write one word on each line.

Tuesday

Example

Today .... was .... the first day of our holiday.

1 We arrived .... the airport late because we drove there and the roads were very busy. After we showed our tickets, we

2 waited for about half an .... and then we got on the plane. I sat next to the window so I could watch everything and Mum sat next to me.

3 Dad had .... sit behind us.

4 When we got to the island .... was four o'clock in the afternoon.

Later we went to an expensive restaurant for dinner.

5 I .... fish then chocolate ice cream!

Part 7

Look at the three pictures. Write about this story. Write **20** or more words.

....

....

....

....

....

....

Part 1
– 5 questions –

Listen and draw lines. There is one example.

Jack   Nick   Frank   Katy

Jim   Helen   Sarah

Part 2
– 5 questions –

Listen and write. There is one example.

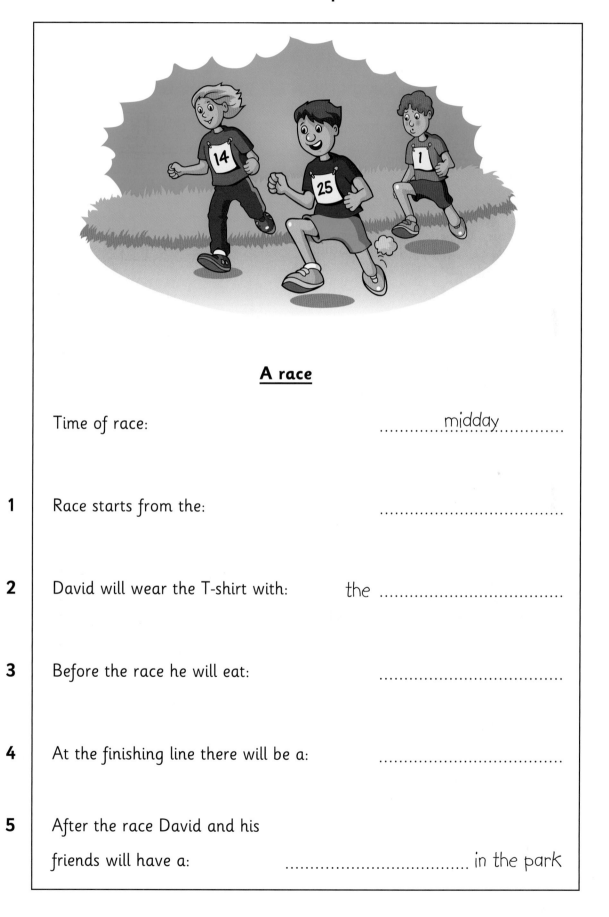

A race

Time of race: .... midday

1 Race starts from the: ....

2 David will wear the T-shirt with: the ....

3 Before the race he will eat: ....

4 At the finishing line there will be a: ....

5 After the race David and his
friends will have a: .... in the park

Part 3

– 5 questions –

What did Mrs Green buy for each person?

Listen and write a letter in each box. There is one example.

Emma | B

Sally | ☐

Oliver | ☐

Michael | ☐

Kim | ☐

Jane | ☐

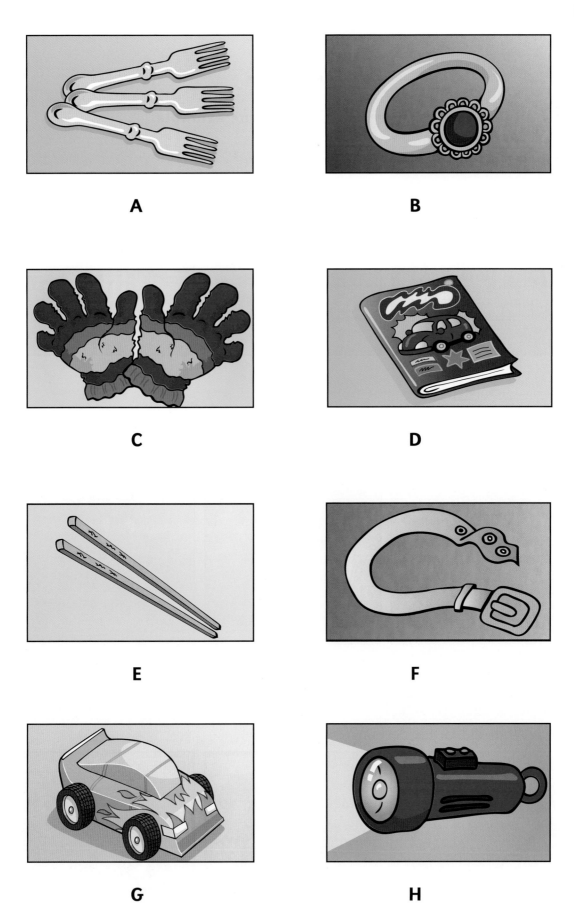

A

B

C

D

E

F

G

H

Part 4
– 5 questions –

Listen and tick (✔) the box. There is one example.

What's the new museum near to?

A ✔   B ☐   C ☐

1 What did Grace like best in the museum?

A ☐   B ☐   C ☐

2 What did Grace do first?

A ☐   B ☐   C ☐

3 What was the film about?

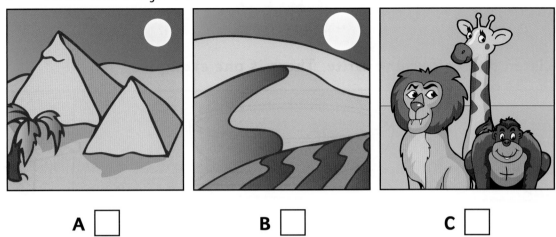

A ☐   B ☐   C ☐

4 What was the treasure box made of?

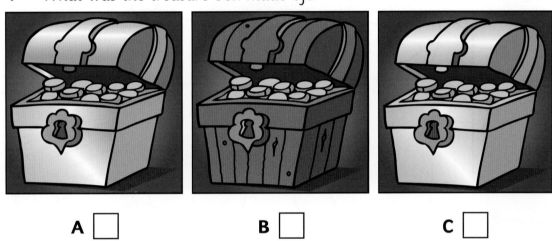

A ☐   B ☐   C ☐

5 What will Grace have to take to class tomorrow?

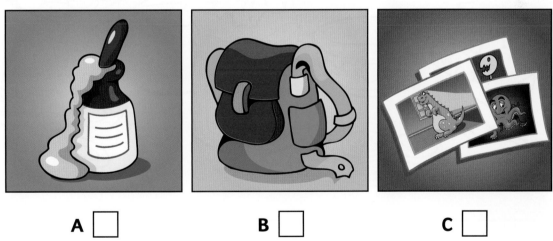

A ☐   B ☐   C ☐

Part 5

– 5 questions –

Listen and colour and write. There is one example

Reading and Writing

Part 1

– 10 questions –

Look and read. Choose the correct words and write them on the lines. There is one example.

a waiter   salt   a comb   meals

sugar

a stadium

a designer

a queen

a factory

This tastes good, and sweets and chocolate are made of it.	....sugar....
1 People make things like bicycles, computers and televisions in this place.	....
2 Go and see this person if you have problems with your teeth.	....
3 You use these to cut food and they are usually made of metal.	....
4 This person is an important woman and in stories she usually lives in a castle.	....
5 People use this when they want to have tidy hair.	....
6 If you want to get on a plane and fly to another place, you need to go to this place.	....
7 This person works in a restaurant and takes food to people who want to have a meal.	....
8 Most people eat two or three of these every day. Breakfast, lunch and dinner are all examples of these.	....
9 You need this if your hands are dirty and you want to wash them.	....
10 You go to this big place to play or watch football or baseball games.	....

an oven

a dentist

knives

an airport

a college   soap

Part 2

– 5 questions –

Michael is talking to Betty. What does Betty say?

Read the conversation and choose the best answer.
Write a letter (A–H) for each answer.

You do not need to use all the letters. There is one example.

Example

Michael: Did you go to the sports centre on Saturday, Betty?

Betty: ....C.............................

Questions

1 **Michael:** What did you buy? Anything interesting?

Betty: ....

2 **Michael:** Which CD did you want to buy?

Betty: ....

3 **Michael:** Oh, I like that one, too. Who did you go shopping with?

Betty: ....

4 **Michael:** Did you go anywhere else in town?

Betty: ....

5 **Michael:** I need to buy some things. Will you come with me one day?

Betty: ....

A	What about next Saturday? I could go then.
B	It's in Station Street. It only opened two weeks ago.
C	No, I wanted to go shopping so I went into town. **(Example)**
D	Mum, my brother Richard and his friend Anna. I like her a lot.
E	Yes, to the bike shop because Richard wants to get a new one.
F	I got a new black jacket and then we went to look for a CD.
G	Anna lives in a flat by the river.
H	It's called 'Remembering'. Sally played it at her party last week.

Part 3
– 6 questions –

Read the story. Choose a word from the box. Write the correct word next to numbers 1–5. There is one example.

Example				
pictures	stairs	pushed	heavy	drove
noisy	finished	news	forgotten	city

Helen's parents bought a new house a few months ago. In their last week

at their old house, the family put all their ....pictures.............. , lamps

and other things into big boxes. Then on their last day in the old house,

two men came and took all the **(1)** .... things, like

the beds, out of the rooms, down the **(2)** .... , out of

the house and into a big lorry outside. Then the family stood for a minute

in their old house and said goodbye to it.

After that, they **(3)** .... behind the lorry

to their new house. It wasn't far because it was in the same

(4) ....

When they arrived, the men opened the doors of the lorry and Helen's dad

walked up to the house.

He put his hand in his pocket and said, 'Oh no! I've

51

(5) .... the key! It's by the window in our old house!'

Helen laughed. 'You always put your keys there!'

'Yes!' Helen's Dad answered, 'but now I must find a new place for them!'

(6) Now choose the best name for the story.

Tick one box.

Mum and the expensive new lamp ☐

Helen and the new lorry ☐

Dad and the house key ☐

Part 4

– 10 questions –

Read the text. Choose the right words and write them on the lines.

Colour

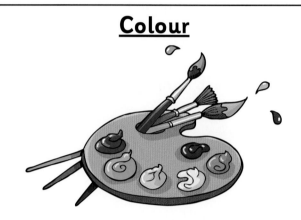

Example   It ....is.............. difficult to think of a world without colour,

1   but try for a minute! There aren't .... beautiful

2   rainbows to look at. You can't choose .... wear a

yellow T-shirt or a blue T-shirt. You can't see the beautiful pink, purple,

3   orange and red colours .... the sky when the sun

4   .... down every evening. What a different world!

The colours of light are different from the colours of paint.

5   .... you mix red, green and yellow light together,

6   they make white light. .... you get brown when

you mix red, green and yellow paint together.

7   Colour is very important to .... of us. Red can

8   make people and animals think .... is 'dangerous'.

Drivers stop when they see a red light and hungry birds don't eat insects

with red wings. Different colours can make you like or hate food too.

9   .... you like to eat blue potatoes or

drink black milk? People have different favourite colours too.

10   .... is yours?

Example	be	is	being
1	much	no	any
2	to	for	at
3	until	in	far
4	going	go	goes
5	So	If	And
6	But	Than	Before
7	much	another	all
8	some	something	sometimes
9	Can	Would	Must
10	What	When	How

Part 5

– 7 questions –

Look at the picture and read the story. Write some words to complete the sentences about the story. You can use 1, 2, 3 or 4 words.

<u>What a surprise!</u>

Last October, Fred and his parents decided to go and stay in the mountains for a week. They wanted to go on long walks there, so they put good walking shoes, maps and all the other things they needed in three big blue rucksacks, which they put on their backs. Then, they caught a bus to go to the station.

They were very excited when their train arrived in the mountain village. It was a cold but sunny day. The grass was very green and the mountains looked beautiful.

That night, they ate in the hotel and went to bed early. The next morning Fred woke up, jumped out of bed and ran to the window. The houses were all white!

'Quick!' he shouted. 'Come and look at the snow!'

Fred's parents were very surprised. 'Snow in October! That's very strange!' they said.

'What are we going to do?' Fred asked.

'Well,' Fred's Dad said. 'Let's get some skis and learn to ski at the ski school here!'

So they did, and Fred loved it. He fell over lots of times in his first lesson but he didn't mind. At the end of the week, he was very good at skiing. His mum and dad were too! It was a great holiday for all of them!

Examples

Fred and his parents went on holiday in the month of
.............*October*.............. .

The family wanted to go on ....*long walks*............ in the mountains.

Questions

1   The family carried all their things in .... on their backs.

2   Fred and his parents went to the station by ....

3   When the train got to the ...., the family were very excited.

4   They had dinner in .... on the first night of the holiday.

5   When Fred got up and looked at ...., he saw lots of snow.

6   Fred's mum and dad thought snow in October was very .... weather.

7   Fred and his parents learnt .... well in the week that they were on holiday.

Part 6
– 5 questions –

Read the diary and write the missing words. Write one word on each line.

	Tuesday, 5ᵗʰ March
Example	There's a new teacher at school and we ....had............. our first science lesson with him today.
1	His name is Mr Hill and .... makes science very interesting.
	Emma and Sophia didn't enjoy the lesson because Mr Hill
2	.... ten questions on the board and they didn't know any of the answers. But I think he's nice!
3	He told us lots .... things about the planets and about our moon and sun.
	We watched a short DVD in his class too. It was about the first rocket
4	.....................................flew in space.
5	I think I'd .... to be an astronaut one day.

Part 7

Look at the three pictures. Write about this story. Write 20 or more words.

....

....

....

....

....

....

Blank Page

Blank Page

Find the Differences

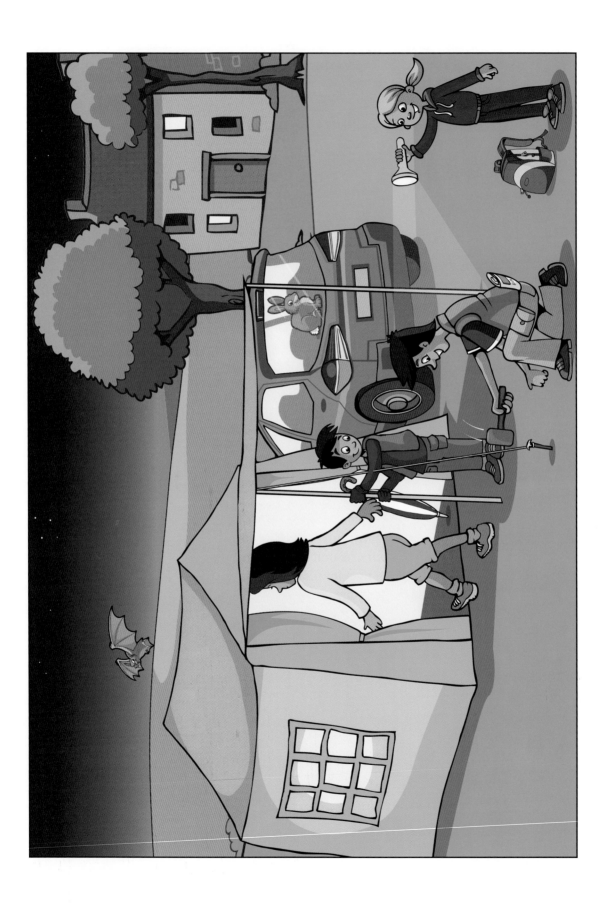

Candidate's copy

Find the Differences

Information Exchange

Examiner's copy

Mary's house

big / small	?
age	?
how many people	?
where / homework	?
colour / front door	?

Tom's house

big / small	small
age	100 years
how many people	4
where / homework	dining room
colour / front door	white

Candidate's copy

Information Exchange

Tom's house

big / small	?
age	?
how many people	?
where / homework	?
colour / front door	?

Mary's house

big / small	big
age	5 years
how many people	8
where / homework	bedroom
colour / front door	blue

Examiner's and Candidate's copy

Picture Story

Betty's birthday party

Betty

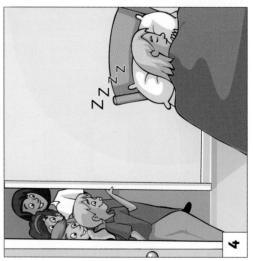

Blank Page

Examiner's copy

Find the Differences

Find the Differences

Information Exchange

Emma's magazine

name / magazine	New Faces
what / about	music
expensive	no
what day / get / magazine	Friday
who buys	father

Charlie's magazine

name / magazine	?
what / about	?
expensive	?
what day / get / magazine	?
who buys	?

Candidate's copy

Information Exchange

Emma's magazine

name / magazine	?
what / about	?
expensive	?
what day / get / magazine	?
who buys	?

Charlie's magazine

name / magazine	Our Planet
what / about	animals
expensive	yes
what day / get / magazine	Tuesday
who buys	mother

Examiner's and Candidate's copy

Picture Story

The key

Sarah

Blank Page

Speaking

Find the Differences

Find the Differences

Examiner's copy

Information Exchange

David's school

name	Greenhill School
where	behind the cinema
how many children	450
what time / start	9.00
sport / play	basketball

Betty's school

name	?
where	?
how many children	?
what time / start	?
sport / play	?

Candidate's copy

Information Exchange

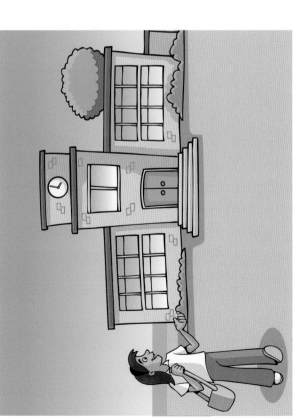

David's school

name	?
where	?
how many children	?
what time / start	?
sport / play	?

Betty's school

name	Park School
where	near the post office
how many children	500
what time / start	8.30
sport / play	tennis

Picture Story

Examiner's and Candidate's copy

Charlie and the elephant

Charlie

Blank Page

Blank Page

Blank Page

Blank Page